PALM FROND WITH ITS THROAT CUT

Camino del Sol
A Latina and Latino Literary Series

PALM FROND WITH ITS THROAT CUT

VICKIE VÉRTIZ

THE UNIVERSITY OF
ARIZONA PRESS

TUCSON

The University of Arizona Press
www.uapress.arizona.edu

Printed in the United States of America
22   21   20   19   18   17   6   5   4   3   2   1

ISBN-13: 978-0-8165-3511-8 (paper)

Cover design by Leigh McDonald

Publication of this book is made possible in part by the proceeds of a permanent endowment
created with the assistance of a Challenge Grant from the National Endowment for the
Humanities, a federal agency.

Library of Congress Cataloging-in-Publication Data is available at https://lccn.loc.gov/2016051253.

♾ This paper meets the requirements of ANSI/NISO Z39.48-1992 (Permanence of Paper).

Para mi familia y ancestrxs—aquí está una humilde ofrenda.

To the first people of all land, everywhere: Thank you for these ways to pray.

I have become intrigued with displaced things—things that are wrong. And translation is in a perpetual state of being wrong . . .

—DON MEE CHOI

I am the space where I am.

—NOËL ARNAUD

Our aim, even in the face of the brutally imposed difficulties of black life, is cause for celebration. This is not because celebration is supposed to make us feel good or make us feel better, though there would be nothing wrong with that. It is, rather, because the cause for celebration turns out to be the condition of possibility of black thought, which animates the black operations that will produce the absolute overturning, the absolute turning of this motherfucker out.

—FRED MOTEN

CONTENTS

ACKNOWLEDGMENTS

Much gratitude to the editors who published these poems, some in different forms, in the following publications:

As Us: "Honeymoon"
bozalta: "This is My Home"
Brooklyn & Boyle: "Lover's Letter"
Cobalt Review: "Already My Lips Were Luminous"
The Coiled Serpent: Poets Arising from the Cultural Quakes and Shifts of Los Angeles: "Postcard to My Father"
Diálogo: "Give Me Your Sister" and "Dream of the Drowned Man"
Entropy: "How Can You Live"
Ghost Town: "Don Mario"
Huizache: "Postcard from My Pop"
Kweli: "La Mera Neta"
Luna Luna: "Pets"
Nepantla: "Agua en Gotas"
OmniVerse: "Fábrica," "The Speed Above," "Portrait as a Couple: México, Distrito Federal"
Párrafo: "What You See, What You Take With You"
Statement: "Palm Frond with Its Throat Cut"
The Volta: "Servicios Pleyboy," "Portrait as a Deer Hunter," "The Apparatus of Love," "Out of the Wreck"

For reading these works in their many forms, I offer heartfelt thanks to: Allison Hedge Coke, Kenji Liu, Juan Felipe Herrera, Angela Peñaredondo, Ashaki Jackson, Forrest Gander, Fred Moten, Derrick Ortega, Allison Benis White, and Maurisa Thompson. For a chance to read and share this work across the country, thank you: David Campos, Lee Herrick, Jen Hofer, Jessica Ceballos, Chiwan Choi and Peter Woods, Karineh Mahdessian, J. Michael Martinez, Maria Elena Fernandez, Natalie Diaz, Iris de Anda, Carribean Fragoza, Romeo Guzman, Joe Scott-Coe, F. Douglas Brown, Mike Sonksen, Sandra Garcia Rivera, and Rafael Zapata. Three cheers to Kristen Buckles for championing this book! And to the dedicated and lovely staff at VONA, the Poetry Center in Tucson, Galería de la Raza, the Community of Writers, Macondo Writers' Workshop, University of California, Riverside, and Bell Gardens public schools—gracias infinitas.

PALM FROND WITH ITS THROAT CUT

PART ONE

WHAT YOU SEE, WHAT YOU TAKE WITH YOU

Already My Lips Were Luminous

My first kiss is with an uncle
    comforting
    me as Amá throws
    up two dollar wine
    after a pool party

I do not know the language of that place
    Sitting on the edge of a cracked red plastic couch
    I am grateful in an ill-fitting girl dress   lavender roses dot the chest
The embrace is short   His breath is two cases of cigarettes and one
aluminum beer
He says good night; the songs of crows
outside unspool
When his sons leave for the Persian Gulf   he kisses them too   and
I'm   confused
    because men never embrace around me   They shove each other's oil hands
into
        car guts and machines that make glass
   Not tender   not soft

   I understand, then   there must be other   ways to love
      your children

What You See, What You Take with You

For Marisela Norte

On the Broadway bus with French diamond lips   and composition
notebooks   Fancy tipped acrylic
    Come closer c h u l a

A chola's dragon   eyebrows scowl at the Walmart

    Old folks' names fade blue on my chest
        Donuts and doctors   and stores   and more   stores

Open a n d c l o s e d   closing   Closer

On dusty cakes   we ride by   the saddest   office in the world
Brown plastic brides and grooms
        The bride's gown is yellowed lace
And the wedding cost more than we could   pay

T-shirts fade in a storefront: Che with m i c k e y m o u s e ears
        He's a churro VIP
A lotería hoodie smothers a boy   waiting   for his quinceañera
sister   to hurry UP ALREADY

Passing the city   college   femur bones are labeled, their names
on   masking
        El Santo reads the news   in the adjacent seat
He's got a modern tuxedo
        Worn down blue boots

On Alvarado, *Alarma!* magazine   another shot
in the head date
        Inky blood   white tile, eye level for Dora and Diego

One bakery morning, a reindeer   and two c h i c h i s tussle at the
register   Baby blond Jesus plays
        his pan d u l c e accordion

On a telephone pole, a bedroom is listed   for a woman or a
Señora, y o u decide

Almost home on the bus, our carriage
El Huracán, that man and his morral

He strolls past the butcher   the fat rolls through electric
yellow Bra straps carve
     into her shoulders

     Los Ángeles is triple x huaraches

Sopping wet pambazos

    Come closer, chula

There's something I've been meaning to tell you

Agua en Gotas

Huaraches , I'm thirsty . A timid leg
The oilcloth mantel , and I want

My hand on her glass of water
She makes me feel like when I lift

My chin , pieces of brute gold will float away
I owe this much

To clay : the cántaro, a jug , a stack of pancakes ,
La olla de café

Hunger is for the chinicuil , his worm , flesh roasted
Chile rojo

He spoke to me in Spanish , so I answered in English
Sprinkled him on my black beans

Her wrists smell of white river rocks , mud ,
To filth , my nails owe

Bits of skin I mark with moons
When she comes up for air to kiss me

I can't stop looking
At her eyeliner

So precise , a machine must have drawn it
I just have to know

That mole , su cuello doblado y exquisito
You're a fool if you think

The answers are only in libraries , but not in me
Cae agua en gotas

How else is water supposed to fall

Servicios Pleyboy

After the Date Farmers

It isn't natural, love that's not seed

Don't play a funeral polka and expect me not to cry
The first ten notes were lemon in my mouth sores
Lemon on my finger-cut heart-slice

> *Did you love him?* my brother asked.
> *Yeah, fool, I did.*

Yes, my pleyboy
He punched the steering wheel—the palm of it—like he'd practiced
On someone before
This because he couldn't find our parking ticket

> *Ey, fool, he's got a bad temper. You better dump him.*
> *Yeah, dude, I better.*

And was it the onions? No. It was the drone of the dead
Line because he didn't always have a cell
And did I love he was mostly phantom to chase what sweet
Remember—the gold high heels, my ass switching, back and forth, back

No AA meeting could patch his drywall holes
No AA meeting could make him stop molesting memory

It was the corn that made us cry, a modified sorrow
It's not natural, a kernel that won't grow
I cried into my taco again today at El Farolito
Leading me away from that dick at constant attention
The jig was up

Born on yellow hills, my pleyboy was a hard climb
A home to mispronounce

> *Fuck that*, said my brother. *There's other fools to love.*

I cried into my taco, and my sailor hat almost fell off

Was it the churros? No. It was the tofu as a meat option

Everybody else cried too
The cashier acted like he was wiping his nose
The taqueros let their salt steam

Was it the chile verde? No. It was the pleyboy
With sweat pants under his jeans—recovering
From a lifetime of being left alone in lettuce fields

I left him too, and what I got left was al pastor

> *Fool, did you get my text?*
> *Nah, ey, my shit is broken.*

What made me cry was my pleyboy rubbing his nose and lips across
My back
And that I wasn't supposed to fuck him

How long can you live in the dark before you get caught?

I cried into my taco because the red tile was rain boot dirty
No matter how hard we scrub
We all came to San Francisco escaping rape
And bullets in the mouth

And that's why everyone cried, not because of me
My brother looked away, out at the street
Families elided pockmarked addicts with no pants on
The oranges piled neatly in pyramids
The bus dangled on driving electricity

Everyone dodging something, even the gabachos
They were just there for lunch, but when we cry, it's contagious
And when one of us dies, they know
They're next

> *Don't be sad, ey. You'll find another fool to love.*

Verde

For Lorca, for C.G.

You are mine once
My hands up, your thighs drugged
with crinoline. Escargot and campos verdes
Verde, que te quiero verde
Well-worn B cups
Your chest, above your ribs
Where your speeding heart lives
And I want to

If you are fucked up, you sober up
To drive me home

You forget a business jacket, ashes
They haunt my hallway for weeks
I smell you in there
A dry-ice potion slinks from under the door, caressing
My ankles when I pass

If our moms could see us now:
Two Hub Cities dykes holding
Back the waters for eighteen million
Put your finger where
Stop it from flooding
The neighborhood, the Food 4 Less
The softball field, my
Daddy's car

Laundromat

After *Lavanderia #2* by Christina Fernandez

It all comes off in here
Inside, an army of washing
Waits to be stuffed
No matter how much mud is on the pant leg, brown
Blood on the panties, underarm on the yellow

Search the machine for that elusive black sock
Its drawn-out color forms its cheeks
Heels mended at least twice

You can't see my face, a woman of ample ass
My head's in the funnel of clean
We watch khakis tumble dry, spotless
Squeaky purple flowers wrap their smell around my neck
Fold up the gossip, leave it in the wire basket bottom
In the corner, a dispenser
Mini Mr. Bubble fizz
Tangerine Tide, baby blue sea
Dollar blouses dangle off the lip and dry

Where we get our peace is no one's fault
It's fine to dig up the dirt on the neighbor
She spends her money on Avon—but it just makes her
more fea, dices tu

¿Pero quién le quita lo bailado?
Not even you
Look through the tagging
White marks, our first works
The sweet stain, the juicy lips

Not a Movie

After Asco's No Movie *The Gores*

Where we live is really space
Mostly monsters and glamour feathers
       Higher metals and helium clusters
            We're heavy spherical—similar to hydrogen
               Spectacular astronomy
Unannounced fires and globular celestials
How nice are we supposed to be?
       Sometimes the door is open
          Mostly it's how it's boarded up
             The gallery wall with no place to hang
               Our ideas tagged with zeros
A film that's not a film follows
We understand stalking and pressing hands
      Does this thing deserve to die?
         Strip this fool, land the platform
Street life is hard to read
But the heart on his shoe
      On my trachea, that's
         Black leather working
           That's what it gets
             For walking, for standing
              In the storefront
This is not a movie
I'm not really gonna do it
      But isn't it fun? Pretending
         Against glass and high heels
            I can't have
If we kill him, what do I get?
How much longer craving vinyl marvels
      Embroidered paper dresses
         A necklace of golden cobras
           With rubies for eyes
             When do I get to sink my teeth in and draw?
I can't kill him anyway
My pants are too tight
      This is not a movie
         It was real, the closed sale

                    The rent dangled high above us
                        I'm just playing, because
Ahead?
There are no more things

Pets

When the chicks were born,   the other woman lurked in her
pharmacist's jacket   Nameless white tufts looking for scraps
         But Amá barked back   at a neighbor's Doberman
The next day, the chicks were laid out on the grass   like dirty
kitchen towels

When our parrot was stolen, the puta was already family,
         hovering
in muffled long-distance phone calls   Dad cruised the Tijuana
         trade route   We dragged orange shopping bags with Amá
What was left of our proud bird?   Two green feathers on the floor of his
cage, uneaten amaranth   Our gate too short to keep out rats

Twin rabbits came to live with us and   humped each other rabid

Dad smuggled diapers in his trunk   The bunnies couldn't leave
their cage to mate   Ashamed to show them to our friends
we covered their cage   The bunnies would not outmaneuver Amá
She recycled them into sopita   Dad's paychecks couldn't feed two houses
My brothers and I sipped the liquid around
the gray flesh, stabbed floating carrot slices   Kept our eyes on dinner

We gave up on pets   The puta lost to cancer   Now a half
sister claims Dad's hands   But her mother isn't really gone
She left
self-assured handwritten letters, crawling in   the attic above our
bedroom   When I flip open Dad's cell phone   I see my half sister's blue
lids, her eye-lined face
She put herself inside for me to see, she's not a ghost
That bitch is real

Dame Tu Hermana

Tenemaktia ueltiutli,* bromeaban los peones
      Tu y tus hermanas en la tienda del abuelo
           ¿A quién se le ocurre pedir así a una mujer?

Entre chismes sobre quien se peleó esta vez, visitaste el ranchito
Se te ocurren sueños, Mamá, y un cuento
      del campo—la bruja se quita las patas
          de noche y se vuelve zopilote—alimenta
             su hija con sangre y magia
                  A veces veo el zopilote circulando. Un
                  pájaro de fierro nos vigila. Con su pico
                  quita la vida, no la da

      El río se secó. Se juntó con el arroyo y en una tempestad
          Se llevó la casa de patitas a la calle
Ya no sabes dónde empieza el terreno de tu tío y
      Dónde acaba el monte
          Los inditos también se los llevó la lluvia
Aunque todavía quedan hombres
      Trabajando en tiendas. Caminan ocho
          kilómetros en chanclas chinas
      para vender veladoras blancas, manteles bordados
con flores color chillante
         Diez pesos por un recogedor, un día de trabajo, cien
A veces, la escoba deja de limpiar
      El agua y la luz se apagan

      Mamá, te da miedo la noche quieta. Para dormir bien, matas
luciérnagas, demasiado esplendorosas
         Muertas nomas son polvo, dejan de alumbrar
Un camino conocido al que no llega nadie más
         Solo queda un airecito nocturno, vigilando
      El azul añil de tu dormir

---

*   En Nahuatl: Dame tu hermana, give me your sister.

¿Que nos queda de esas tierras?
Solo chistes entre hermanas que una vez tuvieron un
Poquito de dinero. A mí también me falta, pero
No se nos quita lo peladas
Es decir, bromea la tía de ojos negros,
No es lo mismo rosa celeste que "rosase el deste"
Frota un pito imaginario, sus manos
calientes de planchar.
Las burlas ocultan lo que falta:
la milpa y el barril, y todo
lo que se pudre

Give Me Your Sister

Tenemaktia ueltiutli
      The workers joke with you, stand in
          grandfather's shop
They teased you as a girl, Amá, the tías, too
      Why would someone ask you
          to give away your sister?

On your last trip home, you caught up on gossip, what
sister was fighting with the other this time
      Sleeping at the little old ranch, you dreamed
          Brittle stories from that land you grew up on—
             the witch who removed her legs at night
               to become a raven
               She fed blood, magic
               to her daughter with her beak

When I'm awake, vultures circle
The skirts of light around the city's teeth
      That iron bird surveys life's worth
          beams its arms, takes breath and does not give life
             The river near your family's land
             Dried up, you say
It joined the stream—the water dragged the adobe
      clear out into the street
          Now you can't tell where your uncle's plot ends
          And where the wild fields begin

          The Indians too were stolen
    A few remain in that store, not your father's anymore
Walk ten kilometers in Chinese chanclas
          To sell lean white candles, tablecloths embroidered with
          shrieking flowers
             Ten pesos for a dustpan
             A working day: one hundred
               Sometimes the broom sweeps without
             water, only light

Amá, the quiet night frightens you
      To sleep well, you kill fireflies, too splendid

But dead, they are only dust, lighting
                        A path no one else knows
                        It is just a slight night air
Watching over your indigo of sleep

What's left of your land, your lighter skin?
                        Jokes between sisters who used to have
                        a little bit of money. I need it, too
                                But we are no less cochinas
                                        That is, says my tía with
                                        the dark eyes
                                polishing an imaginary cock
                        her hands hot from the iron
It's not the same to say "rosa celeste"
            as "rosase el deste"
Teasing obfuscates
            the cornfield and the maguey
Decaying in wooden barrels
            With everything that rots

Postcard from My Pops

¡Mija! You should have been there!
The boxer knocked him out
Like that, flat on the floor asleep
Bien chingón se cree el cabrón

"Me dicen que estoy loco,
Pero estoy loco por ti"

Dance with me, ¡Chata!
No? I'll jig without you then
Whistle whistle! What a riot
Change the channel
More fights are coming on

I wish you were here, mija
Come on, don't get all feelings on me
I may be drunk
But at least I'm home

I could be scrambled
Eggs on the freeway
Or tipsy into the Bufadora cave
Hitting every rock with my face
Making ceviche
Out of me

This Is My Home

I don't want to start off broken   But my pencil is running out
That's OK   We have more lead in the yard

My home is   I can't breathe   Surrounded by sound walls
you   can't   hear
In that quiet, a child finishes their homework,   closing a good thing

The LA River ends in Vernon   After Slauson, the friends of the river run
out, too

The death stench in our water   In our jobs   In the classroom
      Everywhere a gas leak

      This is my home

My mother and brother are ten thousand truck miles   Why won't
their coughs go away?   The freeway, my lover says
      Coffins with windows

      Pig fat rendered into lipsticks
We're bottling the leftovers   Crates of rotten chitlins detonate over
San Marino lawns

When I took Amá to the garden in that city   she looked out the
windshield at their grass and said   *They don't have earthquakes here, do
they, Chata?*
      They do, I said   *They just don't have to feel them*

This is our home: arsenic fairy dust on wedding cookies
      A student plucks a lead bloom that sharpens in the lungs
      Cancer berries cluster and   It's no use, this poem
I lost my parents to the pollution   And no one's come
      to clean my yard

You can have our methane clouds   Windshield tacos
The river is a stream and   the freeway's always running
We are death flower orchards, twenty-one square miles   opening and
closing   Our miscarriages bubble and thin into glue

I've never felt worthless

We plant broken glass in the riverbed   we dream about dabbing lead
perfume behind your clean pink ears   Jumping our skateboards   off
the cement and into your   bright   white
        teeth

My home is invisible wild lupine   blooms purple with tumor pistils
This is our bougainvillea triplex   This is our date palm
This is our jacaranda   This is my home

We stole the whole thing up   That sushi you're eating?
It's cueritos from the Farmer John's
Who are the fools?   Not this nopal light

The student is boiling our water   to get rid of your poison
        The start? The finish?   The PE mile you had to run?
It's here   A river's reverie
        The you and me—
Then   water

PART TWO

LOS ÁNGELES—A PALM FROND WITH ITS THROAT CUT

Palm Frond with Its Throat Cut

After Danny Jauregui's sculpture

There is no one else but me for you / The shape you're in / What are we but lying single surface / subatomics / Your fronds decay / Your remaining life is spiky particles / A golden rot / Don't think / Tilt / You'll want to leave me / But let me smoke you down / The tallow of your heart / Wait to fall / On my body / Aestheticize me / Make me grass

Honeymoon

Paris is full   of dirty   trains
Men who follow me from subways   They're my honeymoon
neighbors
Didn't I tell you?   I married myself

So I'll always   have   company
They live alone   Like me on vacation
They put worn   shoes out on
the sill displacing hours of standing   They want
to talk
Stop   trying
to make   sense   of everything
No parlez-vous français

Paris likes Mexicans   enough   I spoke Spanish before
English, that last resort   The city liked me   enough to let
me   Live off wallabies   bolillos   chocolate   oeufs
I finished the red wine on tap at the galerie

I walked all days   rubbing bronze   angel ears
Reading magazines I understood: queer
feminist   porn   Photographed
myself
with sacred hearts   and   narrow streams   Found Morrison
without his head

That neighbor found   me on a platform
We shared the same black hungry
eyebrows   A woman pissed a fire   hydrant's worth of water toward
our feet
I boarded   hurriedly to other people,   my urban myth of safety

He followed   me home from the train
He did not know
Could not see   If he had asked in Spanish   I would have
gladly flashed him   a marzipan middle finger
The black camera   itched my pocket
So I took his picture   His eyes were closed   I wish I could have
showed him   my giant   heart
His small ideas   those broken clavicles

Portrait as a Couple

México, Distrito Federal

I love you like you are the only one. Between smog-soaked trees, in this city of Vaseline side steps, you tower over. A clean-shaved head, as close to tough as you will ever be. Behind me, the Mexican flag colossal and full. Beneath us, metros shake, pyramids settle.

I am no virgin.

I'm the Aztec God of War. Mouth of relentless ash, the devil at my elbow. I lick flames hotter than your vieja. No sabes limpiarte bien las nalgas, pero ya andas de caliente. But still I hold your hand. Tiaui Mexica. I love you like you are the only one. The last piece of steak in chile verde. The last slice of chocolate flan. That's how you left me, Gordo.

En el zócalo y sola. A creature that can do anything.

How Can You Live

For Iguala and Ferguson

We will sing about the dark times, about school.
About how La Llorona needs a vacation from that riverbed.

Trenches filled across without paper.
And what's fucked is how—

How worn—Che on a T-shirt and Frida is a handbag. What concerns me is
being disposable.

What concerns me are posters of our colleagues, missing girls.
On every lamppost, the buildings are not in heaven, they dream
about us. Dream in a time of war.
It is always a time of war, and what concerns me
is the basilica and no one cared.

How can you live? Citizen and for what.
If we are breath, then bring what is matter.
What concerns me are babies who used to lap
milk now exhale burning hair and skin.

What worries me is that our rights are porous
and we study and read and find what.

Poverty, that's what. Who said? We have when. We have order.

We have a No. We burn it down. Do you see?
There is no paper.
No document can hide the dusk of a grave.
Students are pebbles skipping down that fucking riverbed inside us.

I do not claim the empty notebooks. I am state protected, that handshake
that moves up the arm and begins to feel like kidnapping.

Hearts, what we want, we already have: an e-mail, a loan, a beam. Before
and beyond the colony,
Who can take away what we've already danced?

How can we be left behind when we are what they want to be?
The shine of black leather boots. The sky that great safety—and not guilt—
that injures
What injuries does education breathe?

And in the middle of a punctured lung,
where
is resistance

Resistance as Glass and Lace

After Rosa Rolanda's *Untitled (Glass, Lace, and Butterfly)* photogram

We weren't supposed to make it
Sister—soft spyglass, a cone with curves
You eye a lake, a lilac rose reflection
Cutout flowers for your dead
A doily sky for those   who made it over
Darling electric: What we need are not words
I have stars in my mouth—might you forgive me?
So we can grow and not disappear
Learn to outrun the terrible stories we must
not pass on
I am hunting them down
Oh, sister:
Lo único que tengo son flores

Fábrica

For Dolores Dorantes, Sandra de la Loza, and Boyle Heights

Then we remembered
We are in a drought

And if people don't like it
Que se vayan mucho a la
Fábrica del interior
A procesar
Papeles, submit requests in writing for hearings
Where you won't show up

Because you don't have to
You go wherever the fuck you want
Like water, the lowest road

Finally our dreams don't bite
Finally, we tire of following directions
Finally we break the rules to win
But it didn't matter
It was a project, not a game

A factory imagines our dreams
Otra fábrica
The lover materializes on a monitor
The coming horizon of satellites and wood
Pricey coffee and stupid speakers

There's a plush pink monster sitting next to me
He means well, the macaroni elbow. ¿Codo? Yes
With no thumbs how much harm will he do   can he do   has
he done?
He wants to bring art where none exists, philanthropic condos
His square head is soft, and he's smiling. I know he won't eat me
How many more times will he tangle my understanding?
How does it feel, you myopic spectacle,
To be my throbbing fluorescence?

The monitor is a dying sparkler
And boy do I stink up the place
Here, take these colors I have ready
Crushed eggshells confetti yellow, pink purpled
Que chiquihüite ni que ocho cuartos

Someone take out the trash
Not me. You!
You made my home another factory—for making insides
Another rendering whose smoke means war—

Dream of the Drowned Man

After Lola Álvarez Bravo's *El Sueño del Ahogado*

Scene 1. A sustained walk through mesquite
He might have been a teacher
He was definitely a worker

We found him
Half his face in the dreaming stream
And we are sorry, mostly for ourselves
He's our mirror, a sinking float

Scene 2. Swan Lake *on the Río Grande*
Whoever heard of us
A dozen ballerinas, a gay prince in the water

We brought glass
Water and more thirst

Scene 3. We sit sweetly on bare branches
On stacks of matchbooks
Our crinoline skirts stay dry—we don't approach
Keep our skirts clean

Scene 4. Pobre el que no pudo cruzar
Tantos querer, queriendo
When you crossed, what did the troll charge?
Your money and your life

Scene 5. Ni pobre ni que nada. He crossed over
To this No-Candy Land
This silt in your nostrils with the air sucked out
Windowsill soot nothing can remove

Scene 6. They take photos like this, of men in worn shoes, their rolled-up white sleeves
Of office work. Instead of taking his picture
Why didn't we pull him out of the
Tres Flores glisten?
Why do you think

Scene 7. If he keeps dreaming like this—
Because where would he go
Too much water will
Turn him back
Into the salamander of the inhale

Scene 8. We dance squares into the water
Point out to the wild clouds
To our corner sky, the bridge

Scene 9. His sisters—are home when he calls
Violin strings pluck, and he stands
Takes our hands one at a time
To polka on the bank

Our skirts sweep the shore, trying to clean
This motor oil lake
A puddle of water we sit in
And pretend it's really an ocean

Don Mario

This is his second life
Changing tires, alternating
lightbulb fury

One bedroom in the City of Crowded
Three granddaughters, a limp fixie
dolls with tangled hair, polka dot socks, one
daughter-in-law, a mustached son
Don Mario's bed: a plaid couch, arms
covered in finger filth
In the living room, darting bullets in the dark
The cross-eyed in-law stacks
Dishes, film thick with wait

It's not Acapulco
No one here cliff dives, just swims
bare chested in freeway mirages

Don Mario makes bubbly
cheese pizzas between dominoes
Pictures his neighbor
watering her yellow orchids, tiny ballerinas
Red geraniums obscure her
Grunting husband under a
black Toyota
truck's teeth
taped on with gray masking

Mario dreams of driving
his plump neighbor on her errands
: church first, the 99 cent store
bursting with school kids

He kneads the pizza dough
and pictures her dimpled ass
Not the pimply hemorrhoids
he would get
if his hands could really find her

He saved, borrowed forever, bought a new
White Nissan, a cherry ride
Down Florence Avenue
Itches his mustache
Passes a minimall of Texas Donuts, laid-away jewelers

The morning pizza dough
packed, Don Mario escorts the boxes
to stucco apartments
Shaved heads tip fat
Blue baseball caps exact change
Twenty-four years of gurgling
engines at $8 an hour
Mario knows what he can have

We could be together in secret, he told the neighbor
Why hide? she said. *No,*
we're friends so long
She doesn't need another daughter
who can't wipe her own ass

He stays away, then calls
to ask again
Only the lime tree leaves hear them
A branch bends under
the weight of a chicken
lost on a high limb
eyeing the distance
to the roses below

Girl with Ink and Horseshoes

After *fallin'* by Cruz Ortiz

This locket is a rocket start
Ink ears and here I go, coming to get you
Not get through, but only if you want to

I don't like fallin'
I like maulin'

You still live down the alley?
You dig these nostrils? My sharp shoulders?
I have maudlin songs for your mall job

Come with me, prickly pear
Where I always was, when you're bored
The callejones take me right to you

By all means call me, but you might owe me
What I have is luck
Band shirts and concert tickets
For a singer who plays one song, then leaves
The stage in a huff
Blame it on the weenies

I'm your spring, girl
I love you, my first cactus star map
Let's jam
Away to other skies

I have vessel mileage
Exploding horseshoes
Squeaky brakes?
Nah
That's just how much I love you

Downey Carne Asada

After Shizu Saldamando's *Downey Happy Birthday*

What a silver-tongued father you have, loved   by one and all!
Don't let pigeons sit on you too long   Tie your shoes or nine years' bad
luck   Mami's smoking   She's on break from her Mary Kay lip
gloss   It's time for beers
The Virgen's not missing this party

Me and your mami   We were tender, very tender
Pulled pennies from asbestos ceilings   We left the land of child heroes
Abandoned chromatic gardens
Is this why we came?   For birthdays in a private driveway, pony
rides and jumpy castles

We're tough like that carne asada you gave up   You make me cook soy
hot dogs   that taste like Vienna weenies
At least you love pinto bean tornadoes

Is it hard to make arrangements with yourself?
You waste your coffee-job cash on pints for friends
Friends with bottle-red hair or greased-up pompadours
Those are old dos, from when I was a boy
Don't they know it's over?

I wish I had your wings   This house was not free
The interest a forced closing   It's a Home Depot pyramid scheme
Mr. Holden
How come when I couldn't pay the mortgage, no one took
those bankers' mansions?   How come none of them keep my
nephew company in jail?
Someone should

Mija, if they take your black Mustang graduation   It doesn't matter   I'll
tell the tax man   what I got is pickles
And a fistful of candy   from your smashed star piñata
Is that what I am?   Pay the bills, trim the grass?

Give me that stick   So I can show you how to break things

PART THREE

PORTRAIT AS A DEER HUNTER

Portrait as a Deer Hunter

A lot of heads were bashed [at Stonewall], people were hurt. But it didn't hurt their true feelings. They all came back for more and more. Nothing—that's when you could tell that nothing could stop us at that time or at any time in the future.

SYLVIA RIVERA, STREET TRANSVESTITE
ACTION REVOLUTIONARIES (STAR)

And the paper makes you think this is your land
Like when I lived in Malibu—the grain surf glow

Made me think everyone drove iridescent blue Lamborghinis
I've never been to Malibu. Today is more like summer in South Gate or

Bed-Stuy. A street confettis children in cornrows, trenzas, and bowl cuts
They use umbrellas to shield themselves from the murder of first grade

First grade lined with meth news
Don't be distracted by Supreme Court decisions
The state won't stop shooting, it loves itself over your protection

If I left my lover for the girl who smells like river rocks, within two hours,
the batteries would die on our rabbit-tipped vibrators

I don't want to sit next to her on a plane, the earth leaving below, or discuss
how blackness is not a thing—it's Nothing and therefore Everything   and
I'll blow her mind while she bites a churro

I don't want to show her my mail-order unicorns
Or pick epazote for quesadillas, which I'd cool with my breath
The anchos in the freezer

That strap-on in the closet—a typhoon
You tried to get your boyfriend to let you have girlfriends,
Didn't you?

Jacobo Zabludovsky, pry my eyes from her perfect perfect
Middle finger

The next time you lust for a doctor, show more chichi sooner
Show up to her house with a basket of cookies on a string
Though she's already forgotten your last name

Did she ever know how to spell your first?
Today is not the day to forget that Marsha Johnson and Sylvia Rivera

Hurled the first fists at Stonewall, that they'd been punching everything.
They're still clawing at the sodomy of equal rights

Still trying to lead us home
And yes I will take that girl behind
A blue jay and kiss her like I'm dying!

The time is high and I'm moving on. I'm going to be your number one

Be my woman on the bracket. Save days like halves of the hand
Let's walk into the beautiful garage

Take me out back and show me how to shoot
Be the deer I've always wanted

Postcard to My Father

Under a eucalyptus tree
Mourning doves succor their chicks
And one falls
Hungry from the nest
They leave it there, maybe for later
Dust tracks across my feet

I wish you were here

You wade in ponds of car grease
Elbows bloodied
From scraping against cinder
I'm on vacation, and I don't drink

Pops, you eat the menudo
For both our hangovers

Hold your head up
It's about to roll off

I wish you were here
Napping on a blue-green blanket
Amá popping the pimples on your back

I wish you were so many bottles out of reach

You interrupt last night
And sing a sticky drunk song
"Dicen que estoy loco
Pero estoy loco por ti"
But your song is not about Amá
It's for the one in Tecate

But I'm not a girl anymore
So instead of staying for the encore
I get in my car
And leave

Just like you used to

The Speed Above

For Oscar and all solitary housing survivors

And when I face a window of mountains, trees I cannot name ,
I watch anyway , looking for your shadow
On the wall , your son grows up in photos . First the mole like yours   above
the lip , then the glare into the lens . A picture boy inside wrists . Pacing tiger ,
you are long to your tin cell . Write to life never lasted so alone . This is a
game to keep the hawk hunting . A twelve-year wait of you . Armed and
tedious hours . They civic you first and lose you alone . Your light makes
for rich confinements .   Your son will not letter in your place . Never
watch those mountains . They sink at the speed above solitary . The into
away . You much the list , unloaded .
When a hawk flies overhead I pin this to his talons . This should be your
heels in the silt sinking . Your toes cake with orange earth . You wash with
azure , slide up the oval rocks .
Where you are , you launch a boulder into the lake . You are going to make
it , primo . Sink the dirty jails of business .

Lover's Letter

For Morrissey fans

Because we craved permission to be despondent in English
    Desperate to hide erections for boys
    Behind Trapper Keepers
    To document Kotex leaks in our journals

We needed
    To be maudlin, to be untranslatable
    To do this in private, in the company
    Of someone with rank

We hunted for you in crates, battled mold and being broke
    Scraped pennies from grandparents who collected
    Cans to feed us
    We needed your '50s guitar in the key of sorrow

Mexican and not, born here or not, our duplexes
    South of the 60 freeway
    No Movement murals cushion our daily gray sky
    Our 99 cent interchanges

To your voice, we work our lives away in UPS trucks, as perfect
    Receptionists, in community college forever

This is how you hate the queen
    I seethed at the church for making me dirty
    So we were instant friends

You made me want a public transit death, so we
    Could be together

We saved you from the has-been dollar bin
    We're your American Manchester day dream, empty tire Factories, soot-
    covered eyelids, cracked front
    Teeth and bleeding lips

We fondled open your shirts and built a country around you
    Of sidelong glances and glum gladiolus

When you saw our tight black jeans and creepers
   You could taste our penchant for racing Chevys down
   Slauson with no headlights

We're your wistful twin, that boy you won't share
   You watched us make love in cemeteries
   Made us trim our sideburns, Las Vegas Elvis beats made
   Us jump like beans

We are fatalists by nations on all sides
   Death happy because it constantly raps at our door
   In the carcinogenic heart of this Manchester
   Our black lungs sing with you

Because every time we listen
   It's our last day too

Baby Chihuahua Comes for Your Wig

After *Baby Chihuahua* by Adrian Esparza

> *Girl, if I was gonna come for you, I'd come to your*
> *room at night and cut your fuckin' wigs up!*
>
> BIANCA DEL RIO

We're the same—from royalty's mirrored ceilings—rainbow pom pom
happyfloor realness
    I climb your supple golden
back, cling to your skinny hocks   Sit atop your brow—a ruby
crown—

King of Small Conduits   it's hard to see   what is so bad about
    lollipops from here

    What is so bad about   tanks that skittle across bedrooms
razing cribs   jumping swings   Our bumpy castle   After   BB
hailstorms   We stay by your side

Take us to your leader   It better be a baby   A wax one—with
    Kewpie doll hair twists—a lick of soft serve on her lip
She better listen   She better work

    She better not recall   Governor Chihuahua—he likes us—he's a baby
We're his people

Cake toys   in light blue frosting   We own this white squared
column   It's no diamond mine horizon
    Not tutti-fruiti diapers
    Here, gummy worms writhe   to subway reggaeton   Brown
club kids swerve
    Pink mohawks   swing axes
Slice at the mace—suspended

After the Third Letter, He Writes Back

After Kwame Dawes

I.

Gordo, I stopped by your old house
Figs ripe
In my dress pockets
Navy ferns on the blue fabric

Your mother brought out a plastic tub
Sent her brother up a ladder
To pull down more

You used to call me Fea, a name fanned across
My shoulders

Take these, she said
Shading her eyes, palms slight and shaking
The edges of her hair: copper and silver

I thanked and hugged her
I left again, like I do
And passed the Loveland Street jacarandas
She called my Amá
That night and said
Tell your daughter I love her. Maybe more
Than I had before

I will keep forgiving you, Gordo, for leaving me
For a vieja who thought
You were too much sarape
When all she wanted was tweed

I'm going to keep forgiving you
I wish you'd left me sooner
So I could romance
The girl who took long drags
Of cigarettes in foxholes, who held my
Hand, drunk on too many
Midori sours the color of nuclear apples

II.

Fea. I got your letter
Don't you like your nickname?
I call my sisters ugly too
They're my heart on roller skates

You're not fea—you were a fox with one blue eye
If you were a six when we met, you were an eight
When I last saw you

It doesn't bother me
That you stopped by
You just missed us
My wife doesn't look
Like you: her tits out to there
She hates French fries

It doesn't bother me
That she doesn't want to race, she doesn't need to
We do our thing

It doesn't bother me
This UK, 16-inch megamix apology

You predicted I'd stop loving you—I should
Have said it sooner

Stay friends with my mom—it doesn't bother me—
But I do wish she would stop loving you
So fucking much

Nahuatl—A Revenge

I wish   you would punch him   the way you once hit me
Yek cihua*—tu eres fuerte

He became a pilot, flying a tepostotl[†]   Getting women
Home safely   despite himself
Don't you miss me? She'd moved around his mesh jersey smile

Between oak tree branches, light laces the floor
We let him go to basketball practice

Let that fool pass
We hurry to the oak, stand derechitas yek cihuas

The oak limbs wear delicate xochikoskatl,[‡] necklaces of lichen
Don't you miss me? he asks   She moves around his mesh jersey smile

He told her she needed to lose weight   when he raped her last week
And he follows   A fucked up waltz
Her ex-boyfriend comes out of nowhere   She steps left

My friend and I walk through a school hallway, the tetl[§]
inside of a stone
Between oak tree branches, light   laces   the   floor

---

*   En Nahuatl: mujeres, derechas; straight, women.

†   Avión, airplane.

‡   Collar de flores, flower necklace.

§   Piedra, stone.

La Mera Neta

What is nothingness? What is thingli-ness? What is blackness? [...]
Can there be an aesthetic sociology or a social poetics of nothingness?

FRED MOTEN

I tell my children la mera neta   the real deal about Envy: that mean-eyed
homegirl never sleeps—

Her long red nails break across dark alley schools
For real, don't give her a teddy bear valentine
She'll make you the memory on a snow-white sidewalk
Mylar candle flickering, another boy taken by a gun

She'll chase you because your tattoos are new   Because hers are fading, she
sees county welfare in dirty tones, violet
Lips and wine-dark corn   She burns crepuscular food stamps,
She might pox   your happy bunk bed, cover the ladder   in shattered green
glass that digs into your palms

But Envy is teaching without a class and   I'm   her accomplice,
hiding a taste for metallic learning   hiding
behind books and teachers petting

Our leashes become real when we believe in them
We are fighting the wrong people

What makes us pretty is our taste for fire,   we're self-made
novas, for starting over   broken mirrors   ground to glitter   She is
nothing, people say and step over her

But nothing is something   misunderstood
Homegirls holding hands, black acrylic sparkle
We sit with danger—the one we make—not the one
we are told to fear

The Apparatus of Love

So wonderfully, wonderfully, wonderfully, wonderfully pretty
How did the moon get inside the living room? There was barely enough
room for our bodies

When I rub my hands over the surface, the cave carvings in France feel
Like her necklace, chipped white shell, but how would she suck me?
The carvings, I've never seen them, but I know they're there

Tell me a lie, chula. No, darling, not that one
There's no see that can hold me

You know that I'd do anything for you
The carvings, I've never seen them, but I know they're there

I used her telescope. It was tight and tiny
So wonderfully, wonderfully, wonderfully, wonderfully pretty

And teeming with her breath
Tell me a lie, chula. No, darling, not that one
You can't keep trying to save everyone

But that's how you love best
I will not be kissing any woman behind

A blue jay! I'm done taking care of women
Who don't belong to me

Out of the Wreck

After "The Stranger" by Adrienne Rich

Soy un guerrero de luz   From   my plastic chair   the tallest
tower   watches me back   Directs its   oil pumps
Straight   *down*—a   river   the   freeway
Bare bulbs   light work   for a taquera   All of us
       working   into dawn   where we belong

Straight   *down*—my   river   the   freeway
I walked   *out and*   *back*   to   the   lip   of
the   road
and found   how, under   bridges
mercy   *flowers*   *anger*

But   I follow   the   tail lights   Turn   up the   avenue—*like*
a   *woman*—*like*   *a*   *man*   Turn   what   I   can say
into *androgyne*   , into a   written   room   with   street
walk   sight

And when   *I come*   *into*   *a room*
Some will love my   accent   But   won't   ask   for   papers
I get in   with this skin
Remind   them   *they*   *failed*   *my*   *living*
Their   stories   are   dead—our   verbs   survive

Soy un guerrero   de luz
I sharpen   cities   bare   And when   I   go   where I go
is home   —tiny discos   and tinsel   candles
and   conchas   Y le doy   gracias al   cielo

When I go   language   my   name—the   light   straight
down—I've   *looked before*   My   name is   light
straight   *mercy*—   my
name,   My resist   My   written   room   ignites
the   city   —sharply mist

If   they   ask,   my   name is
written under   *the*   *lids*   *of*   rivers, cities
and   your   dead   .

NOTES

Epigraphs: Don Mee Choi quoted in "A Manifesto for Ultratranslation," "Un manifiesto para la ultratraducción," Antena Books: Libros Antena (Los Angeles, 2016); Noël Arnaud is quoted in Gaston Bachelard's *The Poetics of Space* (1969, p. 137); and Fred Moten quoted from his essay "Blackness as Nothingness: Mysticism in the Flesh," in the *South Atlantic Quarterly*, 112 (fall 2013): 4.

"Already My Lips Were Luminous": The title is adapted from a line in "Homesickness," by Else Lasker-Schüler.

"What You See, What You Take with You": After Marisela Norte's Los Angeles photographs shown at the University of California, Riverside, Writer's Week 2013.

"Verde": Taken from Federico García Lorca's poem "Romance Sonámbulo."

"Give Me Your Sister": The English version of "Dame Tu Hermana" is purposely not an exact translation of the Spanish. Translations change as one moves and these versions say what they mean.

"Postcard from My Pops": After my father came home tipsy one time. The line "Me dicen que estoy loco . . ." is from the song "El Loco" by Javier Solis.

"Portrait as a Couple: México, Distrito Federal": "The devil at my elbow" and the last line are from Cormac McCarthy's *Blood Meridian*.

"How Can You Live": After Benjamin Sáenz. The line " . . . that handshake that moves up the arm . . ." is paraphrased from Chinua Achebe's *Home and Exile*. The poem title was taken from the song and video for "Cómo Puedes Vivir Contigo Mismo" by Alex Anwandter, inspired by the film *Paris Is Burning*.

"Resistance as Glass and Lace": The lines "terrible stories we must / not pass on" are modified from Toni Morrison's *Beloved*. "So we can grow and not disappear": Adapted from Juan Felipe Herrera's poem "I Count Dry Chile Vines and Ancient Leaves," in *Laughing Out Loud, I Fly*.

"Dream of the Drowned Man": The last two lines are from writer Aida

Salazar's author biography.

"Don Mario": After Ko Un's portraits in *Ten Thousand Lives*.

"Girl with Ink and Horseshoes": The lines "Not get through, but only if you want to" and "Where I always was, when you're bored" are adapted from the song "The Loop" by Morrissey.

"Downey Carne Asada": The line "Is it hard to make . . ." is from Neil Young's song "Tell Me Why."

"Portrait as a Deer Hunter": The bracketed words "[at Stonewall]" are the author's insertion. Sylvia Rivera was referring to the riots in particular, but the interview transcription actually reads: "[inaudible]." From "Stonewall Riots 40th Anniversary: A Look Back at the Uprising That Launched the Modern Gay Rights Movement," *Democracy Now!*, June 26, 2009.

"After the Third Letter, He Writes Back": The line "This UK, 16-inch extended megamix" comes from J. Robles.

"Nahuatl—A Revenge": I used the *Nahuatl-English/English-Nahuatl Concise Dictionary* by Fermin Herrerra (New York: Hippocrene Concise Dictionary Series, 2003) for these loose, interpretive translations. They are not perfect, and that's not what I'm looking for; it's the broken parts that matter.

"La Mera Neta": Written with lines from "Ladybirds" by Larissa Szporluk and "Blackness as Nothingness: Mysticism in the Flesh" by Fred Moten," in the *South Atlantic Quarterly* 112 (Fall 2013): 4.

"The Apparatus of Love": Ruth Ellen Kocher's gigan form is composed of sixteen lines of couplets and tercets. I added an additional couplet here. The lines "So wonderfully . . ." and "You know that I'd do anything for you" are from The Cure's song "The Love Cats."

"Out of the Wreck": The phrases in italics are from the poem "The Stranger" by Adrienne Rich. The lines "Soy un guerrero de luz" and "Y le doy gracias al cielo" are from the alabanza "Soy un Guerrero de Luz," written by José Manuel Rosales Álvarez.

ABOUT THE AUTHOR

A graduate of Williams College and the University of Texas at Austin, VICKIE VÉRTIZ grew up in Bell Gardens, California. Her poems have been published in *The Volta*, *Huizache*, *Diálogo*, *OmniVerse*, *Kweli Journal*, *The Offing*, *Cobalt Review*, *As/Us*, and the anthologies *Open the Door* (from McSweeney's and the Poetry Foundation) and *The Coiled Serpent* (from Tia Chucha Press), among many others.

Natalie Diaz selected Vértiz's writing for the 2016 University of Arizona Poetry Center Summer Residency Program. A Macondo Fellow and seven-time VONA participant, Vértiz was the 2015 Lucille Clifton Scholar at the Community of Writers.

Vértiz has taught creative writing at such places as the Claremont Colleges, 826LA, Boyle Heights libraries, public high schools, and at the University of California, Riverside, where she earned a Master of Fine Arts degree in nonfiction.

Her first book, *Swallows*, was published by Finishing Line Press. A first-generation college student, Vértiz is at work on a memoir that reimagines what a real education entails and how it lives in everyone's ways of knowing—as important as any degree.

CPSIA information can be obtained
at www.ICGtesting.com
Printed in the USA
FSHW02n1042080518
47804FS